HOW TO WIN AT LIFE

LESSONS FROM A LOSER

BY DAMIAN G. CUNNINGHAM

damiangcunningham@gmail.com

ISBN: 9798351742717

Published by Unfiltered Pages Publishing House

ACKNOWLEDGMENTS

I am filled with gratitude as I write this. I am so lucky to have such amazing people that have been a part of my journey, and who have encouraged me to write this book. I want to say thank you to my wife, Merricka, who has been a rock for me from the very beginning, I adore you more with each passing year, and my singular prayer is that I get to spend the rest of my life with you, I love you, you are my world.

I also want to say thank you to my closest and dearest friends; Rory, Martin, Kevin, Geoffrey, Andrew... I don't even remember life before you became my friends, and you are all so important to my story that it would have been disrespectful to not refer to you all by name. To my big brother and hero, Glaister. It has been tough growing up in your shadow, but that is only because I am so proud of who you are, and have wanted to be more like you my entire life. To my younger brother Duran, we have not always seen eye to eye, but I would kill for you in a heartbeat, you are loved by so many, I hope you know that. It is because of all of you that I have so many stories to tell, and have the courage to write them. I have only wanted to make you all proud, and I feel blessed every day to be a part of your lives.

I cannot end without saying thank you to Dr. Joseph Farquharson, who assisted me in the editing of this book. Your feedback was crucial to what it has become, and I am forever in your debt.

PREFACE

I was watching a documentary and it started with a man defining hell. He said, “suppose you were to die and you sat in front of God and he shows you who you could have been?” That story cut right through me and has constantly been on my mind. I have always thought that I could have been capable of great things, but I just haven't realized them. I often wonder if I had just made one decision differently, if I could have had a truly amazing life. This book is not about me feeling sorry for myself, it is a series of letters to other people who might be like me: the dreamers, the hopeful, the big-hearted, the overthinkers, the shy kids, the losers that want to be so much more than they are, and the only person that can stop them, regardless of their current situation are themselves.

I have made many mistakes along the way, and I'd like to help others avoid some of them. Life comes at you fast, and you can either spend your time regretting a lot of your decisions or you can decide in a moment to pivot in the direction of the things that you truly want. Sometimes the challenge is figuring out what it is that you truly want, and that will take time. Everyone wasn't designed to know exactly what they want out of life, and that's ok. Sometimes the outliers are the ones that truly have an impact on the world. You may be one of them, let me help you see that there can be so much beauty in your journey from simply accepting that you were meant to be different, and along the way there might be names that get thrown at you; one of them might be "loser". It doesn't mean that it has to define you. If you believe in a God, let it be that when you meet him/her/them, if you are shown who you could have been, you can say that you tried with everything in you to be every bit of whom you were meant to be.

PART 1

Lesson 01

DON'T LET THE DREAMER IN YOU DIE

I remember being 4 years old and hanging out in the guest room of our house. I'd lie there and daydream. . . daydream about flying high in the sky, up in the clouds. It was peaceful and was where I was happiest. Every so often my parents would come and check on me. One day I overheard them having a conversation in their bedroom about sending me to see a psychiatrist because it isn't normal for a kid my age to spend so much time by himself, and what could I possibly be lying there thinking about all the time. It just wasn't natural.

I decided then and there that I'd try to be more social. I didn't like the idea of my parents thinking that I was weird. I felt like a piece of me died then. The daydreamer in me kept me happy, I denied it, and it changed me. I no longer let my mind wander. I no longer allowed myself to enjoy my solitude. I often think if they had just let me be if I would have naturally evolved into a well-adjusted omnivert, who would engage the world at will and withdraw to my happy place when needed. I lost a part of myself that I don't think I've ever really been able to truly get in touch with.

Embrace your inner dreamer, you might discover the greatest things about yourself, your world, and even discover something that could help humanity. That is your time; call it solitude, call it restoration, call it meditation, whatever you choose to call it, make it a gift to yourself in a life that is yours.

Lesson 02

BE YOUR OWN CHEERLEADER

In the fifth grade, I was on the football (soccer) team as a goalkeeper. I liked it and thought I was pretty decent at it. We had a game against a rival school and I was amazing, nothing could get past me. In that game, we won 2-0. Man! that week the phone calls from parents came rolling in. My mom and dad came home every day that week with congratulations. I walked into school every day and was met with so much praise. I couldn't have been prouder or happier. I walked with my head held high and a smile on my face.

The following week we were going to play against the best school in our division. I honestly wasn't very worried, after all, I was an amazing goalkeeper. I'm sure you've already guessed what happened. They shredded my net and the game ended 6-0. It could possibly have been more, but that's the number that my traumatized childhood remembers.

I watched all the parents and kids walk off the field while the other team celebrated. I tried to hold back my tears until everyone left. I'm not sure if I was actually able to. There were no phone calls, no words of encouragement, no pats on the back. Up to that point in my life, I had never felt more alone. I didn't know how to talk to anyone about how I felt. I didn't feel like I had the right to, after all, I was a loser.

I don't know how long it took, but I eventually was able to lift my head high again. The lesson wasn't immediate, but I recognized that people only cared about a winner, and when I lose, I have to be prepared to be my own cheerleader. I have lost many times since, but I've never forgotten, even in the moments when I felt like I couldn't sink any lower, that the only way out of this feeling would be to become my own cheerleader.

The journey of life is challenging, and I think that as adults we forget how difficult it was as children, to navigate a world where our value is determined by how good or bad we are, how right or wrong we are, how good we performed or behaved. And within all of that, trying to figure out who we are, not just a showpiece for our parents to indicate to the world how great they are as parents, or something for them to live through vicariously, but human beings trying to find our own place in the world.

Lesson 03

EMBRACE THE WAY THAT YOU PROCESS THE WORLD

I've always thought my brothers were smarter than me... in fact, I still do think so to this day. I'm a middle child (middle child syndrome in full effect), it was evident to me that they processed and assimilated information way faster than I did and it was incredibly frustrating. I was already dealing with being the "fat" one, and there were no representations in media of the fat kid being intelligent. The fat kids were always slow, silly, clumsy, falling over themselves, etc. I didn't want to be a stereotype, but how do I deal with having a slower brain?

I wanted to be a "smart" kid, I knew that there was some way to get past this hurdle.

I would watch my brothers read something and then read it as well, and to the best of my knowledge, without them knowing, I would ask what they understood. It was mind blowing for me how they just "got it" after just reading anything once. I felt stupid, but I kept trying. I started to notice that with most things, I'd have to read a paragraph 3 times before I understood it. Ok, so that sucks! But at least I knew this about myself, so to keep up I also realized that I had to read faster and for longer. This helped me to understand determination. So my formula became;

Knowledge = (read * 3) + speed + determination

I had to embrace my perceived limitations and take action in the direction of my desired outcome, and this has essentially become my mantra in life. There is always something I can do to be, think, and perform better. I learned a way to embrace the way I processed the world.

Lesson 04

IN TIMES OF STRUGGLE, YOU CAN STILL FIND BEAUTY

I shared an experience that I had many years ago with Merricka (my wife) for the first time, and I thought there might be some value in sharing it with you. I had moved to Barbados while still at UWI... I had found a tiny apartment. My landlord, knowing that I was a student, helped me to get a job with the Caribbean Examination Council (CXC), offloading trucks full with boxes of examination papers and then moving them by trolley to the desks of what was a warehouse of teachers marking test papers. I'd do that all day, then head to school at night. Money was very tight, so for lunch each day I used to make cheese sandwiches.

There were some Bajan students working there as well and I made friends with a few. At lunch time each day I'd find an excuse not to have lunch with them, then head to the back of the building to eat my cheese sandwiches. I was ashamed, I felt incredibly embarrassed, I really didn't want anyone to know how challenging my situation was. Over that summer I got really close to my new friends, my landlord had given me access to a house phone, and one day I got a call that a bunch of my friends were coming to see me. The came over with all this food, we listened to music, laughed, danced, and chatted for hours, in that moment I had completely forgotten about all my financial concerns.

They all left late in the evening, and I went straight to bed. When I woke up the next morning and got ready for work, I opened the fridge to grab the cheese to make my usual sandwich for lunch, I had a fridge full of food, and in my cupboard was bread and snacks.

Without a word to me, my friends had seen that I was in need and decided to hatch a plan to help. When I went to work that day and saw them, I couldn't help myself, I was in tears. In my time of struggle, I was able to see and experience so much beauty from the love and care I received from essentially strangers. I am grateful to this day, and for the rest of my life for the kindness shown to me. I have never been back to Barbados since I left, and I've never seen them since, but I carry them in my heart with me every day. I often forget that there are beautiful people in the world, but when I reminisce on that experience all those years ago, it helps me to believe, and I know I try to be a good person because of this.

If any of my friends from this story read this article, let me say thank you again. I am a better person for having met you, and I try to do good because of you... I am forever grateful.

Lesson 05

NEVER WALK AWAY FROM THINGS YOU LOVE

I started my career in sales working for what for me was a truly prestigious company and what felt like an amazing opportunity (even though the contracts back then weren't great). I loved my job, I loved my customers, and I loved the feeling of accomplishment I had every month after meeting my targets. It was challenging and fulfilling and I felt like I belonged, for the most part. Eventually, I got a new boss and over time, it felt like I couldn't do anything right. I was young and naïve.

I figured if my boss had issues with me then I must be doing something wrong. At the time, my targets were being met, my customer reviews were positive, and my event execution was on point. I just couldn't understand why I was under so much pressure. I was losing sleep, stressed out, and demotivated. I loved my job, but what felt like undue pressure had just become too much for me. I decided that the best thing for me to do was to start looking for another job. I thought that I was young, I could get another amazing job, and I could be happy somewhere else. I found a better-paying job and moved on. Sometime after, I spoke to the assistant of the company's National Sales Manager and she asked me why I left. She told me that there were plans for me to be promoted and that everyone was surprised that I had moved on. Not even three months after I left my dream company, they fired the boss that was making my life a living hell. I thought about reapplying but talked myself out of it. I often wonder what my life would have been like if I had practiced what I now know to be "grit" if I could have potentially made it to the top of the organization.

People will come into your life, and it may feel like they are blocking your path, but your world is bigger than just one person or a few people, who instead of seeing your value, may decide to try to hinder your growth. Never forget your value, never forget that you have something special to offer, and never lose faith that your ambitions can be realized right where you are.

Lesson 06

ACKNOWLEDGE YOUR VALUE...*even if you are the 7th friend*

I consider myself very fortunate to have the calibre of friends that I've been able to associate with: business owners, CEOs, directors, consultants, etc. I revel in the types of conversations and interactions that I've been able to have. I've learned so much, and continue to learn from these champions within their chosen fields.

Recently, I was able to have a few drinks (as is customary) with about 6 of these friends. As usual, the conversation was scintillating, we talked about leadership, personal development, strategic thinking, politics... I went home that evening elated and sad at the same time. I was so happy to have been able to sit at that table and be filled with knowledge from these men that I see as true leaders, but I was the "broke friend", and that hurt.

It made me think about my entire life and how hard I've tried various endeavours but never been able to truly improve my financial situation. I've seen in my friends' eyes how they'd like to see me win, and I honestly believe that if they could, they'd help.

A few days later I had a drink with one of the gentlemen from that previous group interaction, and I guess it was the alcohol but my feelings about that previous evening came out. He said to me "Damian, there are a few things that you need to recognize. I think you are the smartest one among us, I don't know anyone who feverishly seeks knowledge the way you do, and the other thing that you didn't realize was that you are the true common denominator in that group of people that were together, we were all there because of you".

I sat back, I tried to focus on what he had just shared with me, and I allowed myself to smile. My value is so much greater than what's in my bank account. Yes, like everyone else, I want to be financially free, and I still believe that I'll figure it out, because like my dear friend said I "feverishly seek knowledge". Take comfort in what you genuinely bring to the world, and never diminish the value.

Lesson 07

JUDGE NO ONE

My Dad and I were having a conversation once about how people tend to be judgmental of others and empathetic to themselves. He painted the following scenario for me:

Imagine that you are standing at the buffet line at a hotel, and you are there with a friend and you see a man hit the buffet twice. You might say to your friend, "Wow! That guy is greedy!"

But if you had hit the buffet twice, you might say to your friend "The food was so good I had to have another plate."

People tend to treat themselves with empathy but others with judgement. Judge no one.

Lesson 08

DECIDE YOUR WORTH

Believe it or not, I used to think that when a company made an offer that it was really what they could truly afford to pay. So, I'd accept roles that were way below my desired salary and would intend to prove to them my value by increasing the revenue and profitability of my area/division. Then after doing so, I'd have the confidence to go in and negotiate my desired salary.

So, I'd start, push myself as hard as possible to surpass targets, build the requisite internal and external customer relationships, and live and breathe the brand(s). But then, when I felt that I had done enough and had meaningful talking points for me to go in and renegotiate my salary, I'd go into the conversation with very little confidence (because in my head I'd always be thinking that they could easily replace me, I'm nothing special).

I wasn't confident, and they could smell it, so I'd get the usual spiel i.e. current economic climate, inflation, cutbacks, etc. and

I'd walk away from the conversation defeated, depressed, and frustrated.

I repeated this action several times over several years always hoping that someone would just choose to invest in me the way I invested my time, attention, effort, and even my heart into the company. I couldn't understand why my friends and colleagues seemed to be advancing but it just wasn't working out for me, but as we already know, I was walking into each situation doomed to fail because I hadn't decided my worth. If you don't know your worth, others will decide for you, and chances are that they'll undervalue you. Make a conscious effort to determine what kind of salary you want to truly earn, because it will also guide your thought process as you venture into entrepreneurship. If you think you only deserve to earn $1000 then you'll never see the $1,000,000 opportunity. Decide your worth.

Lesson 09

THE ONLY MASTER IS HOW YOU PERCEIVE TIME

I am amazed every day by how people lose sight of the fragility of their existence. But somehow we all buy into these ideas of reaching certain goals at specific times in our lives: degree, house, car, marriage. So we spend our lives on a timeline, bargaining with the universe for our desired achievements. I am not advocating for people not to pursue their goals. I am just protesting against perceived timelines, primarily because once a timeline isn't met, it dictates that the goal isn't achievable and then the goal is discarded.

If we were all able to recognize that the trajectory of our lives is not preordained and that the timing of wins in life is not absolutely in our hands, then we could recognize that the only master is how we perceive time. If there are goals that matter enough to you, then their achievement is what should truly be sought and not a societal or cultural expectation of achievement within a given time frame.

Your goals, the ones you truly care about should not have a time limit but must be pursued relentlessly because, without them, you would have missed out on a life's purpose, not an itinerary.

Lesson 10

CLEARLY DEFINE YOUR IDEA OF SUCCESS

(happiness never lies in material possessions)

Generally, when someone says that they are successful, immediately we think of financial achievement, and it is understandable because financial success has both quantitative and qualitative attributes. If someone is a millionaire, then we know statistically that they control 43.4% of the world's wealth (quantitative), we also know that millionaires are able to afford a quality of life that would generally be desirable by most. The assumptions are; less stress because they can afford all their bills, they can afford to take luxury trips, they can afford the best restaurants, send their children to the best schools, etc. (qualitative).

I don't know about you but I would love to be rich. I have come to the absolute realization that at least 80% of my current issues are related to the lack of money. Why do I worry about bills? The lack of money. Why do I feel inadequate? The lack of money. Why do I feel unsuccessful? The lack of money. I have started and failed at many businesses and projects, and I am tormented by that ever-illusive dollar amount that would change my life for the better. I am constantly anxious about my financial situation and how to get out of it. Everything I have done in my life was at some level my attempt to bargain with the universe for financial success. That's why I went to university, got a master's degree, started businesses, and worked on projects with others. Everything was with the hope that I could achieve financial success. I eventually became so focused on this "lack" that I was missing out on so much of the abundance available to me.

The amazing relationship I have with my wife, my immediate family that I love dearly, the incredible friendships I have, my health, the fact that I still believe that my life can significantly improve. There is no reason that you can't be grateful for your life and still strive to have a better one. Make the time you need to evaluate your ideas of success, engrave them in your mind and strive towards all of them. Your life is far more than a dollar amount, and true happiness never lies in material possessions.

Lesson 11

CHOOSE LOVE... *always*

I had just come out of a 3-year relationship that in my opinion had drained me emotionally, mentally, physically and financially. I remember when I met the young lady, I was at a place where I thought that what I wanted was a stable relationship, so I went all in even though there were several red flags. I was so committed to making it work. I'll spare you most of the details but if I hadn't taken the decision to end the relationship, it would have meant to me that I had lost complete self-respect. Nevertheless, that relationship left some scarring, so for the next six months, I dated occasionally, had no interest with connecting with anyone on an emotional level, and the mere suggestion of a relationship would lead me to ghost whomever had suggested it.

Labor Day also happened to be the birthday of a dear friend, we had made plans to hit the gym in the morning and grab some breakfast after. He had mentioned that he was going out with a group of mutual friends that evening but I wasn't feeling it, so

I declined. We did our workout and then went to a popular local restaurant for breakfast, I saw a beautiful girl there, had a quick chat, got her number and made plans to have dinner with her the following night. I was having a pretty good day so far. The birthday boy and I ended up at my best friend's house (who was in the crew going out that night). They ended up convincing me to go out with them.

That evening as I got ready, I still didn't want to go, but I'd already made the commitment, so I jumped into my car and went to the venue, when I got there it was 6 friends that got out of my best friend's van, including Merricka. Merricka was a girl that I had met through my best friend almost 10 years earlier, we had dated briefly, but at the time she had just broken up with her boyfriend and they were kind of going back and forth, so we decided that we were best as friends. We stayed friends all those years, seeing each other at the occasional party, club, etc. I would see her and often wonder if we could have been something, every time we saw each other the conversation was amazing and I truly had always thought about her as someone special. But when I saw her that night I was so nervous that I hugged everyone except her. She looked at me and screamed, "Damian Cunningham yu nuh si mi?!" We laughed and I hugged her. I felt something spark within me. We headed into the lounge and just started talking and laughing, had a few drinks, and eventually realized that we were holding hands. It felt like one of those now or never moments, I decided to ask her out, so I said "Would you have dinner with me tomorrow night, or has that ship sailed". "The ship never left the dock," she replied. I smiled what I'm sure was one of the silliest smiles and we decided that we'd figure out the details in the morning.

I was excited about our date, and hoped that it would go well; the plan was dinner and a movie. We went to dinner that night and the conversation was amazing. We talked for what felt like hours. At the movies I don't think we ever stopped holding hands and when I dropped her home, she let me kiss her at the door. I drove home incredibly happy. I could think of nothing else but her. I asked her out again the following night, and the night after that, and the night after that. All I could think about was her. The only person I wanted to be with was her. Two years of dating and six years of marriage later and nothing has changed,. It's still her.

I could have chosen to be a broken person after my last relationship. I could have let myself be consumed by someone else's brokenness, but then I would have missed out on the love of my life. I chose to let myself love and be loved, and it's the best decision I've ever made in my life. Oh! By the way, the girl that I met at the restaurant on Labour Day. . .I never called.

PART 2

Lesson 12

STARTING AT STUPID

At a very early age, I became fascinated by human behaviour. What made people tick, what motivated them, what demotivated them. People became an ongoing social experiment for me. One major thing that I noticed was people's fear of looking stupid, and most would avoid it at all costs, to the point where they wouldn't even allow themselves to ask questions for fear of looking or feeling stupid. In this regard I already had an unfair advantage, I had never thought of myself as being particularly smart, so I guessed that I had nothing to lose by asking questions.

I would more often than not preface my questions with "This might be a stupid question but...", and I'd get the occasional chuckle if it did turn out to be a silly question, but the vast majority of the time I found that the question was well received and even considered valid. So I got good at starting at stupid because there was no way for me to learn, grow and develop if I was afraid of starting as a novice. I'm not good at most things, but I know this; because I have tried a lot of things, and I'm ok with that, but one thing I won't do is not try. I consider myself, from a general knowledge perspective, a very well-rounded person, I have talked to everyone and anyone that would entertain me, because I always felt there was something I could learn from starting at stupid.

Lesson 13

SHUT UP!... *and be the most interesting person in the room*

As a child, I felt like we either had a lot of parties at home or we went to a lot of parties hosted by my parents' friends. I was very shy, so I spent a lot of time pretty much hiding behind my dad and listening. There were so many cool things that I noticed, like some of my uncles were super funny and would hold court, people would surround them and there would be jokes and belly laughs and I wanted to be like that, to be able to hold the attention of a room and be, what I thought at the time, adored.

There was one uncle that was always there; handsome man, always well dressed, appeared to be quiet but always seemed to be having individual conversations. I tried to analyze the difference in personalities and wanted to know more, so when I could, I'd hover at his feet. I picked up that in conversations that I heard him having, he said very little, it was mostly one-liner questions and the occasional laughter at the responses.

Every conversation though, seemed to end with a hearty handshake or a hug, then a big smile and I would always hear the other party to the conversation say, "It was great talking to you".

I started wanting to be more like him, he was able to create relationships with very few words, he seemed more appreciated for his wisdom than his ability to make people laugh, he was received by all with an expectation of feeling better about themselves by having shared a moment with him. It took me a while (as most things did) but I eventually got it, his value was in his ability to get people to talk about themselves, and nothing seemed to make people happier than talking about themselves.

They felt connected to him because he provided an outlet to expression that isn't always readily available. I've tried to assimilate the best of both worlds. In a crowd I am motivated to entertain, but in one-on-one conversations, I want people to feel heard, to be understood, and in that way to always feel validated.

Lesson 14

YOUR LOGIC SHOULD BE MALLEABLE

If a friend comes to me with a business idea, and I have a difficult time visualizing the process of it working, I tend to say, “I can’t see it, but if you have the vision, it’s not important if I do”. The greatest gift that anyone can give to themselves is self- belief, I think it is Henry Ford that is credited with saying, “whether you think you can or you think you can’t, you’re right”. Your belief in yourself can lead to extraordinary results. There are so many examples that we can point to: Elon Musk, Steve Jobs, Mark Cuban, Jeff Bezos... all these men have one absolute characteristic in common, self - belief.

Each dared to challenge the status quo to create empires, and along the way, they all encountered people who told them that it was impossible. Logic should be malleable, there are ever evolving examples of why it should be, humanity once believed that the earth was flat, and why shouldn’t they? It was sound logic. Humans once thought that it was ridiculous to fly, the Wright Brothers sure changed that.

I get mad at myself every time that I think about doing something and talk myself out of it, because if there's one thing I know for sure, is that I'll never know unless I try, and more importantly, I have several examples in my own life of things that I just decided that I was going to do and they worked out, and more often than not in those scenarios, I didn't spend endless amounts of time trying to gather other people's opinions. I just went in with faith, determination and consistent effort. If there's a formula for achieving a goal, I think that's it;

Goal Achievement = Faith + Determination + Consistent Effort

I think if there's any goal that you've achieved you might agree with me.

Your brain is designed to keep you safe from anything that is uncomfortable. Your mind will give you a myriad of reasons why you shouldn't do it, and as Visu Thembekwayo would say, "all of the excuses are valid, but do they allow for progress?". Your self-limiting beliefs can be damaging. My mentor recently said that if you grew up in a house where your parents constantly said things like "we can't afford that" or "it's too expensive", then you might grow up believing that money is scarce and therefore you'll always have limiting beliefs on access to or earning a lot of money. That one cut right through me, because I know that I struggle with my belief that I can be rich. . .but I'm working on it because my logic is malleable.

Remember being a child and thinking that anything was possible? Life and society may have beaten it out of you, but give yourself the opportunity to believe again that anything is possible for you, embrace the joy of feeling like you can have anything you want in life, because maybe you still can.

Lesson 15

ROUTINIZE THE PAIN OF GROWTH

Most of my life has felt like a roller coaster: high speed, lots of ups and downs, twists and turns. I have recognized through it all that what I call my "highest self" tends to emerge from difficult situations. Even when I feel like I'm at my lowest, there's always a voice inside of me that wants to believe that I can figure it out and make my way through it, mostly because I have faced several challenges and overcome them before.

This is why we need to choose to routinize the pain of growth. I've been working out for most of my life, more often than I'd like to admit, I just don't feel like it. I chose to create a morning routine for myself; get up at 4:45 am, brush teeth and wash face, make a cup of coffee, read for 15 minutes, get ready and head to the gym. On the mornings that I don't follow the routine, it is so much harder to make it to the gym, I find all kinds of reasons why I can't make it that day, and this is mostly because

I have deviated from the routine behaviour that I rely on to get me out the door and to the gym.

Everything that we deem as worthy in our lives come at a cost, and your choosing to embrace the pain, stress or difficulty associated with your goal may make going through the situation more palatable. The early mornings, the late nights, missing out on fun with friends and family, all have to be a part of a much bigger plan to make life more meaningful, not only for yourself but also for those you love.

It is stupid for a man to wish for a life without challenges, because they are inevitable. It is far better to choose to routinize the things that form a part of your daily life that represent challenges, especially once you recognize that will lead to you ultimately having a better life.

Lesson 16

DON'T CHASE FRIENDSHIPS, BUT ACKNOWLEDGE THAT YOU HAVE AN OBLIGATION TO FOSTER THEM

I have an unspoken rule for myself, that is, if I think about someone more than once during the day, I'll reach out whether by call or text. I've realized over time that there's incredible value in this practice. Communication and connection are necessary aspects of being human, and if you are able to maintain positive relationships and create meaningful connections, then you have created a powerful network for yourself.

I have worked as a Business Development Manager more than once in my career, and what I believe has been my greatest value has been my ability to gain access to people of influence, usually through a prior connection to the individual or someone being willing to give me access, and this only exists because I have made a concerted effort to foster and maintain friendships. I never allow thoughts like "he/ she never reaches out to me, why should I call?", to influence how I choose to interact with people. Once I perceive the relationship as having value, then I don't allow my ego to get in the way.

Everyone is busy with careers, family, and ambitions of their own. I think it would be narcissistic of me to believe that others would or should spend too much of their time thinking about what's going on with me, so I reach out whenever I can. I don't chase friendships, but I acknowledge that I have an obligation to foster them. These personal and professional relationships can serve you for a lifetime. Enjoy the process of creating and maintaining them, they will enhance your overall life experience in ways you are yet to imagine.

Lesson 17

BE AUTHENTIC...*even if it leaves you misunderstood*

I've never quite felt like I belonged. . . anywhere, and for a very long time I thought that if I played the role of the "cool guy" that kinda went along with the flow of things, it would allow me to find a place in the world. It didn't. I spent most of my time feeling alone in a crowd, I would leave social situations and replay in my mind the interactions, and lambasted myself if I had said anything that made me appear awkward or strange. This left me with constant anxiety.

I hated feeling alone. I hated the idea that I disliked who I was. There had to be a way to exist in this world and feel connected and be authentic. I decided to spend some time on my own, engaging my thoughts and perspectives, enjoying the beauty of my mind. I discovered that there was no malice, no hate, no desire to cause harm. I only wanted to love and be loved.

That was enough for me. I knew I was a good person. I knew I wouldn't be happy unless I was my authentic self and I recognized that the friendships that would always and only matter were those that encouraged me to be myself. I am a weird guy, I live in my head and I don't quite fit in, but I am me. I love ferociously and I am indifferent to most, but that's ok. Be authentic... even if it leaves you misunderstood, you are here to live your life, not to be understood.

Lesson 18

MOST OF YOUR RELATIONSHIPS WILL BE SUPERFICIAL...*and that might be a superpower*

It's always felt as if I vibrate on a different frequency from others, but that left me with an overwhelming desire to connect. So I'd actively attempt to foster friendships even when things didn't feel quite right. Many of these people eventually failed me as friends, and I realized that I shouldn't have tried to create these relationships anyway. After some introspection, when I look back on a lot of these so-called friendships, they were incredibly superficial and over time I'd even forget that the person was ever a part of my life.

So that got me thinking even more about how I choose to interact with the world and came to the realization that it's ok to have a lot of superficial relationships, as long as your intent is to not mislead anyone into believing that there is a deep or meaningful connection. I'm allowed to put people in my designed superficial relationship categories; for example, one category is "people that I'll have a drink with and entertain conversations".

When I see these people we can have a drink, a laugh and even scintillating conversation, but once the conversation is over, we can completely move on with our respective lives until we meet again.

Being able to put the vast majority of people that you meet into categories of superficial relationships allows you to recognize that their opinions of how you choose to live your life is irrelevant, and so you are free from any social norms or constructs that you might think you need to adhere to in order to be accepted. Living absolutely on your own terms because you are uninhibited by the opinions of the masses is a superpower. Your greatness can never be determined by how other people see your life but what you actually choose to do with it. Enjoy your superficial relationships, because those are the ones that set you free.

Lesson 19

OBSERVE THE NARRATIVE OF YOUR CIRCLE

When someone is attempting to make a positive change in their lives there is so much that is involved in the process. It starts with recognizing that the way things are don't quite fit with who they want to be (that might be a subconscious experience). Then there is a realization that if they want to move in a particular direction that there needs to be a change. They start to visualize the change, then there is an acknowledgement of the process involved in executing the change, then they begin the actual work of implementing the change. This requires consistency of effort which over time becomes habit.

Change has occurred, and there is a letting go of the old methodology that they once used. That internal struggle is hard enough, though what I'm about to discuss should never be the primary focus. It will undoubtedly affect people in the process of changing/evolving. What is the narrative of your circle?

Quite often when people are attempting to make changes in their life, they look for external support and validation from their peer group. Many end up realizing over time that they are probably going to be a “one-man band”. This is mostly because who you were before the change could easily accommodate the peer group that you belonged to. If you’re trying to improve your diet, and what your friends typically want to eat is junk food, it’s highly unlikely that you’ll be able to influence the entire group to go to a restaurant with healthier options. The combination of habits and group think will definitely make your task a difficult one. You may be ridiculed for wanting to make a change, or even face attacks from people who think you “believe that you’re better than them”.

You should take none of this personally because when you’ve decided to make a change in your life, YOU HAVE DECIDED TO MAKE A CHANGE IN “YOUR” LIFE, and that’s ok, and it’s also ok that your peers may not understand it...yet.

Change is uncomfortable, it may mean cutting loose some of the people who were actively a part of your existence. But if you are to make real change in your life, it is critical to observe the narrative of your circle and act accordingly.

Lesson 20

YOUR CLOSEST FRIENDS MAY NEVER BE YOUR GREATEST SUPPORTERS

You'd think that if you decided to start a new project, go back to school or start working out that your friends and family would be your strongest supporters, and why wouldn't they be? They are called your "support system" for that very reason, right? But many times the exact opposite occurs, your family and friends aren't very quick to jump on the bandwagon. Even more interesting, maybe even surprising, is discovering that quite often amazing support for your endeavours comes from people on the periphery of your life.

Why is that? Well, have you ever heard the saying "familiarity breeds contempt"? The people that are closest to you know too much about you. They know your failures, your shortcomings, your quirks and this can have what is referred to as the Horn Effect. The Horn Effect refers to the idea that the negative aspects of a person, as identified by an observer, are interconnected and potentially perpetuate themselves. So if your friend has seen you fail several times, they will assume that you'll probably fail in the future.

The opposite may hold true for people on the periphery of your life. They don't know you and they get to enjoy whatever snapshot of you they might have, which is the Halo Effect. The Halo Effect is the tendency for positive ideas and opinions of a person to positively influence other perceived aspects of a person. So for example, if the observer sees the other person as attractive, they may also assume that they are intelligent.

What I hope you've realized by now is that either observer, whether influenced by the Halo or the Horn Effect is forming opinions solely on their perceptions which may have absolutely nothing to do with your reality. So it is advisable to take either with a grain of salt and focus on your own feelings and emotions related to anything you'd like to achieve. Do you my friend! Because to do anything else has been proven to be meaningless.

Lesson 21

WORK HARD... *and then let people know you did*

My parents instilled a very strong sense of humility in us as kids. You were expected to work hard, keep your head down and eventually you would be noticed and rewarded for your efforts. So throughout most of my life, when I'd see business professionals, scientists, lawyers, etc. speaking boldly about their accomplishments, it made me uncomfortable. In my eyes they were boastful, conceited, and narcissistic. Why would you feel a need to "show off" in this way? At the time I just didn't understand it.

In a perfect world, my parents would have been right. Your hard work and effort would be recognized by your superiors, peers, friends, and family. But that just isn't real life. My parents' philosophy worked well for me initially. Being a shy kid, it was great being able to just do what was expected and fly below the radar, but there was something inside me that wanted more.

I'll never forget what one of my favourite teachers (Mr. Barnes) said to me in the 9th grade while I was handing in a paper. He said "it's easy to get through life hanging out at the back of the class. It's much harder and more rewarding to let yourself be seen". I struggled with that statement for years but took it to heart regardless.

The simple truth is this: people are too busy trying to figure out their own lives to notice what you're doing unless you're willing to show them. The best CEOs know that their "real job" is marketing their product or service. Work hard. . . and then let people know that you did. The examples are in our faces everyday: Jeff Bezos, Bill Gates, Elon Musk, Steve Jobs, Ariana Huffington. They all understand/understood that in order to stand out, you have to be willing to let the spotlight shine on you. Never be afraid to market yourself and recognize this as an ongoing process in any chosen field. You can be great at doing something, and/or you can be known for being great at doing something.

PART 3

Lesson 22

IT'S OK TO PLAY SCARED

I had the good fortune of having a conversation with an incredibly successful entrepreneur. He shared his story with me, and it was amazing! I asked him how he was able to manage his emotions when taking on new projects. His response has completely shifted my thinking about those who are truly financially successful. He said "Damian, I do deals in the hundreds of millions of dollars, I put my family, my shareholders, and my business at risk all the time... I'm at the dentist constantly because I grind my teeth, the anxiety is ridiculous!... but I have to do these things because it's what makes me, me"

I thought about the things that I do in my life that are anxiety inducing, and how minuscule they are in comparison, but I acknowledged that they are "my things" and "my journey", and so I shouldn't try to make a comparison. The lesson is in acknowledging that it's ok to play scared, nothing great has ever been achieved with average thinking and/or average effort. I'm constantly pushing myself to get comfortable with being uncomfortable, it's frustrating but even more so exhilarating. I encourage you as I always encourage myself, do the things that scare you most, there is so much beauty on the other side that will make it worth it, even if you're unable to see it just then, you will eventually.

Lesson 23

IN TIMES OF STRUGGLE, YOU CAN STILL FIND BEAUTY

I shared an experience that I had many years ago with Merricka (my wife) for the first time tonight, and I thought there might be some value in sharing it with you. I had moved to Barbados while still at the university, I had found a tiny apartment. My landlord, knowing that I was a student, helped me to get a job with the Caribbean Examination Council (CXC) offloading trucks full of boxes of examination papers and then moving them by trolley to the desks of what was a warehouse of teachers marking test papers. I'd do that all day, then head to school at night. Money was very tight, so for lunch each day I used to make cheese sandwiches.

There were some Bajan students working there as well, and I made friends with a few. At lunch time each day I'd find an excuse not to have lunch with them, then head to the back of the building to eat my cheese sandwiches. I was ashamed, I felt incredibly embarrassed, I really didn't want anyone to know how challenging my situation was. Over that summer I got really close to my new friends, my landlord had given me access to a house phone, and one day I got a call that a bunch of my friends were coming to see me. They came over with all this food, we listened to music, laughed, danced, and chatted for hours, in that moment I had completely forgotten about all my financial concerns.

They all left late in the evening, and I went straight to bed. When I woke up the next morning and got ready for work, I opened the fridge to grab the cheese to make my usual sandwich for lunch, I had a fridge full of food, and in my cupboard was bread and snacks.

Without a word to me, my friends had seen that I was in need and decided to hatch a plan to help. When I went to work that day and saw them, I couldn't help myself, I was in tears. In my time of struggle, I was able to see and experience so much beauty from the love and care I received from essentially strangers. I am grateful to this day, and for the rest of my life for the kindness shown to me. I have never been back to Barbados since I left, and I've never seen them since, but I carry them in my heart with me every day.

I often forget that there are beautiful people in the world, but when I reminisce on that experience all those years ago, it helps me to believe, and I know I try to be a good person because of this.

If any of my friends from this story read this book, let me say thank you again. I am a better person for having met you, and I try to do good because of you... I am forever grateful.

Lesson 24

YOU'RE GOING TO SPEND A LOT MORE DAYS WORKING THAN CELEBRATING

We all know that no one is an overnight success, but when most of us think about the person that we admire or want to be most like, there is a tendency to dismiss the hard work that led to their level of success. Every motivational speaker or coach will tell you that it isn't all about hard work. Let's face it, your dream could be to be an astronaut, but if you spend your entire life working hard as a janitor, that won't make you an astronaut. Your energy has to be focused absolutely on the goals that you're desirous of achieving. But be mindful of the fact that the journey is far more meaningful than the destination.

There are so many goals I have set for myself at different points in my life that when achieved left me thinking "now what?". But I think that if you are a naturally driven person, what you'll eventually have to realize is that what you're feeding within yourself each day is your drive to achieve, not the actual achievement.

I recently set out to complete a 6-month Project Management Program in 2 months. I did it! When I got my final grade at 3 a.m. after pushing myself day and night for those two months, I was left feeling incredibly unfulfilled, I went to bed with that thought of “now what?” because I felt nothing. I was in a sombre mood the following day, unable to understand why I wasn’t revelling in my achievement. I asked myself why I felt this way and then I had a moment of clarity. It has never been about the result, but about finding the will to achieve the goal. That is where the beauty lies, and for that reason, if you are a naturally driven person, you’re going to spend a lot more time working than celebrating.

Lesson 25

YOU CAN'T POUR FROM AN EMPTY CUP

I believe that everyone should seek out financial success, academic excellence, and garner as much social currency as possible. These pursuits in my opinion can have significant positive effects on the quality of your life and that of others. I don't believe that your interest in achievement in any of these areas negates your ability to focus spirituality.

That being said, I am often surprised that the following stereotypes still exist:

- to be wealthy means that you must be ruthless;
- to be an academic means that you are pompous;
- to have social currency means that you must be vain.

If you stop and think about it, the things that can truly help to move society forward from an individual perspective require the following:

- you can't give back to society in a significant way (financially) unless you have achieved wealth;
- you can't pass on knowledge if you haven't sought and acquired it yourself first;
- you can't garner support for any worthwhile (social) pursuit without having social currency.

You can't pour from an empty cup neither literally nor figuratively. So for those that aspire to achieve in any of these areas and are motivated to have a positive impact on their community, I salute your resolve to create duality in your life.

Lesson 26

YOU ARE NOT AN IMPOSTER

We live in a world that expects us to be perfect. If you don't agree with me, check out your own social media presence. We don't post our most vulnerable moments, we post the highlight reel of the amazing experiences that we can share with family, friends, and colleagues.

No wonder there are so many people walking around with what's referred to as "Imposter Syndrome" which is essentially the feeling that you will eventually be exposed as a fraud related to your experiences and accomplishments.

Fraud or not, the facts are that more people than you think feel this way. Some of the most successful people that you interact with struggle with believing their hype, and it's completely understandable. When you accomplish things, people only see the highlight reel. They'll never see the sleepless nights, the fear, and anxiety that was involved in the process of getting to success.

When someone has achieved success in one area or another, society automatically deems this person an expert in their chosen field. they are praised for being successful, and an authority in the area of perceived expertise. In actuality, most people are just able to push through the fear long enough to find success, and if asked to endure the entire process of getting to success again, probably wouldn't.

No wonder people struggle with imposter syndrome, the very idea that because you have been successful, you should always be successful. That just isn't real life.

I recently decided to learn to code. It's something that I've been thinking about trying to do for a long time, but I was afraid to start and not follow through. I feared that if I ever told anyone that I was learning to code and then I fell off, that I would be seen as a failure, an imposter.

What a silly waste of energy in the opposite direction of what I wanted to achieve. Why would I be afraid of someone knowing that I had tried and failed? The real failure would have been to have never tried at all. Unless you're faking your way through life, you're never an imposter. You're just a human being trying to figure out your place in the world.

Lesson 27

THE FEAR OF FAILURE IS NEVER GOOD ENOUGH A REASON NOT TO TRY

We are in the middle of the COVID-19 pandemic and the catch phrase at the moment is “the new normal”. No one really knows for sure what that means and I genuinely believe that, whatever it is, we haven’t gotten to that point yet. We are still in the transitional period as the world adjusts to life in this pandemic.

Whatever “the new normal” is, the facts are that life has and will continue to change for most of us. And those feelings that come with change are expected: fear, anxiety, anger, frustration, etc.

What we know for sure is that life must and will go on. How we choose to respond to it will be one of the greatest determining factors in who will thrive going forward and who will fall by the way side. We’re already seeing several people and companies adjusting to life as it is right now and some are doing really well simply because they've already accepted that the way we lived our lives or went about doing business has to evolve (even if only for the short term).

Many people and/or companies will get stuck in analysis paralysis, completely unable to move forward with any course of action because a chosen path may present the potential for failure, but all paths have that potential.

Now is the time to get those creative juices flowing. What we know is that after every recession there has been an upsurge in people and companies coming up with and executing great ideas that have led to great success.

Microsoft, Apple, Airbnb, and Netflix all found success after a recession. None of them would be the companies they are now if they had remained stagnant. The fear of failure is never good enough an excuse not to try. Why be afraid to fail? As Russell Brunson says, "failure isn't something you own, it's something that happened". I encourage everyone to take a chance on yourself, your ideas, your goals, and your dreams. Today, embark on whatever creative journey you need to so that your life can be better tomorrow.

Lesson 28

GET COMFORTABLE TALKING ABOUT MONEY

For most of my life, I used to say "I don't need to be rich, I just want to be comfortable". I know, that just screams, "loser!". I was cool with saying that because most people around me would concur but I have realized that that statement is a cop out. It's a way of justifying your life as it is; a way to never have to truly push yourself to work as hard as you would need to, to get to your definition of "rich". It is a way for you to "live in gratitude" because your life isn't as difficult as most people. I'm not suggesting that you can't live with gratitude for what you already have; however, you can live with gratitude and still feverishly pursue lofty financial goals.

Cash rules everything around us, and even if you consider yourself a minimalist, if there are simple things that you enjoy like going to the beach (all beaches aren't free), drinks with friends, the occasional dinner, going to the movies, all these things are not cheap. And if the baseline for your standard of living includes what I think of as these basic things, then you'll need money to be able to do them all. Get sick and you'll realize how quickly everything you have can disappear in the blink of an eye. I no longer want to be around people that don't want to be rich, I don't want to be affected by their complacency or nonchalance. I'm still not where I want to be financially, but everything in me is still trying to figure out how I can get to my financial goals and build my dream life. Get comfortable talking about money, whether it is when you're negotiating your salary, having conversations with your significant other about finances, or joining an investment group.

Whatever it is, make money a priority; not your only priority, but a priority. Take it from me, I have a lot to be grateful for, and most of my existing issues in life could be fixed with money. It's great that money is my only real issue right now, but that's because I spent so much time working on my marriage, my friendships, my education and somewhere during all this work, I took my eye off money, and I am trying to fix it. If you're anything like me, you should be trying to fix it too.

Lesson 29

WHEN YOU FEEL AN ITCH, SCRATCH IT

It was a Friday night in late 2011 and as usual I was at a popular night club, with people, but alone with my thoughts. I was looking at the same people, having the same conversations, and I was bored out of my mind. I had been thinking for a long time that I needed to inject something new into my life if I wanted my life to improve. I had gotten used to being the party guy, the fun guy, the guy with a drink in hand and the welcoming smile. It had become my identity so much so that people would see me and talk to me about a party that they saw me at, and how much fun it was even though I hadn't even been there. Work, party, work, party; that had become my life and I had become sick of it.

I had always enjoyed learning and I had been thinking for years about doing an MBA. I figured with my current trajectory, life would just be more of the same unless I did something to propel me further, and I was aching for a more challenging career and the ability to earn more. I decided in that moment that I had thought about it for way too long and it was time to take action.

I had been looking at schools for a while and at the time, believe it or not, I was already enrolled in an IT programme at a local university, but I was only doing it because I felt lost. When I was younger, in response to me saying to my dad that I wasn't certain what I wanted to do with my life, my Dad said "Until you know what you really want to do, just do something". That kind of became my mantra, whenever I felt lost, I'd do something, anything to not feel like I wasn't going anywhere.

The university that I was studying at had recently started offering an Executive MBA programme, and I went straight there that Monday morning and picked up an application form. Over the next couple weeks there were interviews and eventually I got accepted into the programme. I had JM$530,000 saved at a Credit Union, which was pretty much all the money I had, I requested a manager's cheque for $500,000 made out to the university and handed it over. That was roughly a quarter of the cost of the programme and I thought to myself, "the rest will figure itself out". Those were two very hard years. I lost a job, my relationship fell apart, my IBS got worse than it had ever been, I had difficulty sleeping, and my weight gain was ridiculous. But within all of that I was able to graduate with a 3.91 GPA and couldn't have been prouder of myself for making it through.

Whenever you get that nagging feeling within yourself that there is something that you should be doing, I think that it's the universe trying to direct you towards your true north, towards your goals and dreams. If you have an itch, scratch it.

Lesson 30

EVEN THE GOOD YOU DO IS STILL ABOUT YOU

How do you define yourself? If you define yourself as a "good person" then more than likely you will do things in order to justify that identity. There will always be actions that you inadvertently take in order to validate how "good a person" you are. I can understand that for some people this statement might make them uncomfortable, because they like the idea of the good they do being about the other person in need of the help.

How many times have you done some form of "good" for others and either basked in the glory of how good a person you are or at least felt the need to share the experience with someone else unsolicited? We all want to feel validated, that we matter, that we matter to others, and usually the easiest way to do that is to do good for others so that we can be liked.

The reason that I felt it necessary to highlight this idea is because if you really gave thought to the "good" that you do, maybe you'd do a little less. Not because you are a bad person, but because you have become more intentional about your actions and interactions. Ask yourself the question, "Am I doing this to be seen as a good person or am I doing this because I genuinely care about the well-being of the receiver of the good deed?". Chances are, more often than not, it's to validate being good. I am not advocating selfishness, I am advocating self, meaning that we all need to take a closer look at our own existence and how best we can serve our lives and the lives of those we truly care about.

There are so many people that steal from your energy and resources because you choose to accommodate them. Quite often the answer needs to be "no", if only for your own peace of mind. I don't expect this thought process to be immediately accepted. But ponder on these things if you feel that they could potentially make your life better.

Lesson 31

YOU BECOME WHO YOU CHOOSE TO BE THROUGH REPETITION

I have struggled for most of my life with thinking positively. It feels to me that I've been on a roller coaster ride of being able to believe in myself and do the things that I truly want to achieve, and then feeling completely useless and unable to be or do anything that can change my life for the better. People that have known me long enough will tell you that they've seen my weight fluctuate significantly. That is primarily because I developed an unhealthy relationship with food at a very early age. The short version of that story is that whenever I felt vulnerable, sad, or lonely, food was my go-to for a shots of dopamine to feel better, and inevitably I'd feel bad for overeating.

I realized that I wasn't very happy with being or feeling fat and recognized the only way I could change would be to change my thinking about food and more importantly myself. I have gone through extremes in body transformation and the motivation changed at different stages of my life. What I have identified as the common thread on my roller coaster were the thoughts and behaviours that were being repeated in each period of my life. When my thoughts are flooded with negativity, I am prone to overeating and missing workouts. When I focus on the positive things in my life, I tend to work out regularly and make better dietary decisions.

So instead of punishing myself for times when I feel negative thoughts taking over, in an attempt to change my state of thinking, I choose to do the positive things that help to change my thinking. I go for a walk, I seek conversation with a good friend, I push myself to just get into the gym. Essentially, I use my body to change my mind. I don't always win, but the big picture thinking is that if I do that more often than I don't, then I can maintain a generally healthy weight and lifestyle.

You are what you repeatedly do, and if there is a version of you that you truly want to be, then the only real choice is to consistently exhibit the behaviours that will lead you in the direction of that version of you that you would most like to identify with. Even if you are only able to act in the manner of the best version of you, and you still don't truly believe it, taking action over time will help get you there.

Lesson 32

MAKE ADVERSITY YOUR FRIEND

In March of 2020 I was furloughed. I wasn't incredibly worried because I still had another job (for most of my career, I've always tried to maintain at least 2 jobs), but I was very aware that the COVID-19 pandemic was going to have an inevitable and significant impact on the economy, and my ability to earn. I knew I had to do something to generate additional income and by that time most people were panicking about what to do. I tried to avoid those people. I needed to have a clear head to focus on what I knew and what might be possible.

I went to see a friend of mine at his workplace. Business was dead so we could have a normal conversation outside, it was super quiet, there were literally no cars on the main road. I wanted to figure out what I could do to get through this rough period without too much financial stress, so I was throwing ideas at him, then I remembered something a customer of mine had told me years ago. I was the Sales Representative for a prominent liquor distribution company and she owned a duty-free liquor store. We had developed a very good relationship and I always enjoyed talking to each other. One day in a conversation about the industry she said to me “Damian, let me tell you something. Liquor will always sell. People drink to celebrate and people drink to forget”.

In that moment, I decided I was going to sell liquor in a pandemic. I told my friend the story and told him that I was going to try it. He was sceptical, and I understood, but I wasn’t deterred. I called a friend who was a major wholesaler in western Jamaica, and told him that I wanted to start a home delivery liquor business. I told him that I was going to work with small margins because of the current economic climate and I’d need preferred pricing from him if it was going to work. He agreed, we confirmed prices and I began advertising.

When I sold my very first bottle, I said a prayer of thanks and asked God to keep this going, because if I could make a few thousand dollars a day, it would help to keep us going. At the time, I really believed that the pandemic would be over in a few months (yeah right!).

More than a year later, the liquor business has not taken off, but it has helped a lot in keeping us afloat and even able to have fun at times, we saw a lot of other people truly struggling, so I was and remain infinitely grateful to have had the idea and follow through with it. The lesson for me was that in the face of adversity, it does not help you to worry or cower in fear. Make adversity your friend, embrace the challenge and ask yourself questions. Your brain is designed to provide you with answers.

Lesson 33

EMBRACE YOUR GREATEST FEAR

My greatest fear is that I will die insignificant, having achieved nothing and having had no real impact on the world. It has taken me a very long time to understand that I am happiest and feel most fulfilled when I am in service to the people I care about, and at my core I care about humanity. My biggest reason for writing this book is that if by virtue of someone having read this book, their life is somehow made better, then my personal suffering would have value.

I have read many times over that the best way to live your life is to think about your death and what you would want said about you after you're gone. What better way is there to find the value in your life than to embrace your greatest fear? When you push past your excuses, all of which you can find ways to validate, the truth is that a life worth living is one in which you have given your all to be who you believe that you were meant to be. Anything else is just you sitting on the side-lines of your own life.

Hey, I haven't completely figured it out for myself; however, if this book represents my greatest accomplishment, then at least I took the initiative to write it. Embrace your greatest fear, push past your self-limiting beliefs, dare yourself to be the best version of you. If you win or lose, who really cares? In the end your life is absolutely about you so don't ever allow yourself to be an extra in your own movie.

PART 4

Lesson 34

RELEASE THE DISAPPOINTMENTS OF THE PAST

It was 4:30 am and I was on my way home to Montego Bay from a promotion in Westmoreland, driving through Whithorn, lights on bright and barely able to keep my eyes open. I hit a pothole, hard! I knew something was terribly wrong with the car because I could barely maintain control of the steering wheel, but there was no way I was stopping. It was my third promotion of the night. I had worked my way from Montego Bay to St. Ann and back through to Westmoreland. Saying that I was exhausted would be an understatement. I heard a ping on my phone, looked at it and saw that it was an email from my boss. He wanted to have an 8:00 am meeting. I waited until I got home and sent him an email explaining the situation and that I'd be in office as soon as I was able to figure out what happened with my car.

A few months earlier I had accepted the role of Brand Manager for a new line of energy drinks. I was excited, the energy drink market was booming and I had a massive catalogue of ideas on how I would be a major player in the market with a lifestyle brand that would transcend all major demographics. When I met my then boss, he sold me on a vision for the brand. I was in! I recognized that I had difficulty defining a vision of my own, so I comforted myself with the belief that maybe my role in life was to help someone define theirs.

I decided not to go to sleep. I called my mechanic at 6:00 am and he was able to get the requisite parts to fix the car. I got to the office by 9:00 am. When I stepped into my boss's office he immediately said "Mr. Cunningham, I told you I wanted you at the office at 8:00 am, why didn't you take a taxi?". I decided then and there that this was not the type of person I wanted to work for. I quit a week later.

This is just one of the many examples of times in my life where I had bought into someone else's vision and had been disappointed by either who they were, how they approached the situation, or even their own willingness to support what they said was their vision.

My friends are probably tired of hearing me say, "This could be an amazing opportunity", because at the time of each opportunity I truly wanted to believe they were. I have had to fight the feeling of brokenness that multiple disappointments can create, but I also continue to believe that life can change for the better in a moment if you keep believing and trying. Don't ever let disappointments of the past influence how you perceive the future. The past is not a prerequisite. It has no place in the determination of your future. Release it!

Lesson 35

FIND A HEALTHY OUTLET

Depression was a part of my life long before I had a word for it. At a very young age I found myself being sad about many things that I knew were beyond my control. I discovered that I would get momentary relief when I ate things like sweets and chocolate, and so I indulged. I got fat and that made me even more sad. I would eat when I got sad, then I'd get sad because I over-ate.

I hit high school and like most teenaged boys, girls became the focal point of my existence. All my friends were getting girlfriends, but I was the shy, fat kid. So there wasn't a lot going on. I got invited to most parties because I still ended up having popular friends, but I was a wallflower. I saw people dancing, and having a great time and all I could think about was those movies where you'd see the fat kid doing some stupid dance and being laughed at by the popular kids. That wasn't going to be me.

So I just tried to avoid any situation that would embarrass me. I shared my feelings with my closest friend and he made the most direct and cliché statement, he said “if you want to lose weight, just do it”. Somehow it resonated with me. I decided to start my body transformation journey with walking home from school every day. The journey was about an hour.

One evening while I was walking home from school, a girl stuck her head out the window of a taxi and shouted in my direction, “Fat bwoy! Stop nyam yu taxi fare!” I was so embarrassed. I think I ran all the way home, and hid in my room and in my thoughts. But I resolved to not have anyone make me feel that way again.

That summer my mom got my dad a weight bench and some free weights. It became my weight bench. I worked out literally morning, noon and night. I had become obsessed. Besides lifting weights, I had to do at least 1000 push-ups and sit-ups each day. I went back to school after that summer feeling like Superman. I felt confident, dominant, unstoppable. There were still many unresolved emotional issues, but I had found a way to address one of my issues and I grew to love the benefits of exercise.

To this day I still struggle with my weight, but exercise has been a consistent part of my life for the last 25 years and I intend it to be for the rest of my life. The motivation behind it has changed from time to time, but I lean on exercise for stress management, confidence, health, testosterone production, and general well-being. Find a healthy outlet or two, or three. Consider making some form of exercise a part of your lifestyle. The benefits over time are infinite.

Lesson 36

FEEL THE BETRAYAL, FORGIVE QUICKLY

I had an idea for an online business. I started working on and writing out a proposal. I kept the idea to myself because I believed that there was a real opportunity there for me to create something of my own. Somewhere along the way, a close friend came to me with an idea that had many aspects that were similar to my business idea. Seeing that I trusted him, I decided to share with him what I had been working on. He was excited and we made the decision that we were going to work on the business together.

I was adamant that this was going to be the opportunity that was going to change my life. I had all the right relationships and connections I needed to make it a reality. We agreed and brought in a friend of mine that was a tech genius, so now we were three. I was able to gather the necessary data needed to create the website. It was going to be revolutionary! I started to let myself fantasize about my new life, how I could create something with real value. I would finally have something that would truly validate my existence, and I was passionate and ready to see it through.

We started off really well. We set meetings initially for Tuesdays and Thursdays of each week, and I made it my responsibility to draft all company documents and manage the project. After a couple weeks, my original partner in business started to miss meetings. First was either a missed Tuesday or Thursday then it became weeks. We had completely lost momentum. My level of frustration was through the roof because I wanted to get this business off the ground, but I also wanted to maintain our friendship, and at the time I was uncertain how to communicate how I felt without feeling like I might cause irreparable damage to our friendship.

It took me a few weeks but then I mustered the courage to have the conversation that we needed to have. I told him how unhappy I was with the lack of interest. I told him that if this was something he really wanted us to act on then he needed to step up his game. He didn't take the conversation well and we didn't speak for about two weeks. The project was now completely stalled.

He called me one day and said that he wanted all the project documents. I asked him why and he said that he wanted them because his plan was to continue without me, because the project was entirely his idea. That made me mad, but I held my composure and told him that there was no way I'd be handing over my work to him. We ended the conversation and essentially the friendship in that moment. I don't think we've spoken since. I still love him and still think of him as a brother, and if he needed me, I would be there. I forgave him years ago. I knew that any anger that I carried would only eat at me (lesson # 1), and beyond this one infraction, he had been a great friend. There was no reason not to love him because he let his ego get in the way of our friendship (lesson # 2). I was incredibly hurt, so I decided to feel the betrayal, but forgive quickly (lesson # 3).

I haven't looked at the documents since. Similar versions of the business exist today, not the same model, which to the best of my knowledge is yet to be created. I often wonder if I should revisit the idea, but somehow it feels tainted by how things ended between us. Friends will fail you; it is a given, but forgive them, because you might need them to forgive your transgressions one day.

Lesson 37

FREE YOUR MIND FROM SELF-LIMITING THOUGHTS

There's a part of me that has always thought that I could be great. At what specifically, I am yet to determine. I allowed myself to fantasize about the possibility that I might be some kind of savant, and I would eventually stumble into a situation or role in which I would shine so brightly that I would be recognized for my genius. Well. . .no such luck.

When I look within my immediate circle, there is so much success that it is almost maddening. Where is that door that I need to step through? Or that switch which I need to flip? Or that glass ceiling in my mind that I need to break through in order to find myself among my friends and colleagues that I so desperately want to identify with? I have spent a great deal of time trying to identify what are the traits of those that find success and what truly differentiates me from them. I've worked really hard all my life, so it can't just be about working hard. It can't be the friends I've chosen, all of whom are successful in their chosen fields. Maybe it's environmental. If I moved to a new city or country then I'd have a better life. But I'm here and other people have made it. Can't I grow where I'm planted?

The one truly distinguishing factor that I have identified is belief in self. I have always wanted to achieve amazing things, but I never quite believed that I could. I have read tons of self-help books, listened and watched hundreds of podcasts on self-belief. I could probably motivate anyone to achieve their goals, that is, everyone except myself. There is this underlying feeling of unworthiness that has plagued my existence. I often feel like my greatness could be found at the next turn. Somehow, I just have not been able to make it around the bend... yet. I'm sure that there are people reading this now and feel very much the same. Not everyone finds their passion or purpose early in life, the key is to keep searching, learning and exploring. Never let yourself forget that you can be absolutely amazing at something, don't get caught up in the illusion of time, you can still find your place in the world as long as you maintain a positive attitude and keep believing that you can be better.

Lesson 38

EVEN WHEN YOU'RE LOST, YOU'RE STILL SOMEWHERE

If you're like me, it's hard to look at life without wondering if you're on the right path, especially if you think you've made several wrong turns along the way. You look in front of you and what you see is a road full of jagged rocks, the path is dark, the fog is thick. Anxiety builds up. There must be danger ahead. There's no way that this isn't another wrong turn.

Most of us were raised to believe that life is linear. Go to school and do well, get a job and work towards being promoted, save as much as you can and eventually enjoy retirement. For some people, that plan works. Our societal construct in many ways allows for it to work. However, the world has changed, the economy, job stability, the nature of jobs have all changed. But unfortunately, the mindset of people have not changed along with it. There is still an expectation that you should just pick a path and run with it until your dying days. Sounds awesome, right? Of course it doesn't, but it is safe, supposedly secure, and for most it's thought to be the right thing to do.

What I find interesting is that we all know that the people that change the world are not those who followed the roadmap, but those who decided to forge their own path. They took the path with the jagged rocks, the path that was dark and foggy, and we always celebrate and revere the ones that win. On the other side, those who take the path but don't find what society deems as success are considered failures. Don't you see how stupid that is? Nothing about life comes with guarantees besides death, but we allow ourselves to believe that there should be guarantees.

What actually happens is that we have a generalized idea of "hope" based upon a collective belief that if we do "X" then we will get "Y". For those that choose the uncharted course, there is what I believe is a greater belief in self, because there is a path that can be created to bring about the life that is being dreamed of. Isn't this just another form of "hope"? Those who choose the uncharted course should always be celebrated, because they decided to step into the darkness knowing that even though they will be lost, they are still somewhere, and that is the only way to create your own destiny.

Lesson 39

DON'T BE NAÏVE ENOUGH TO BELIEVE YOUR BEST WORK WILL BE YOUR FIRST ATTEMPT

My friends have been encouraging me for a very long time to write a book, and even though I've been writing articles for years, I was very afraid of what writing a book would signify. I would be opening up myself to a world of criticism. Suppose the book doesn't resonate with anyone? Who cares what Damian has to say? What qualifies Damian to give advice? The book might not do well. All of that energy being dedicated to what is essentially a first attempt. No one gets on a bicycle for the first time and expects that they'll be doing wheelies immediately (or if they do they'll get a rude awakening in the form of cuts and bruises).

So why would anyone believe that they should be guaranteed success at any first attempt? Life is only exciting if you keep having a lot of "firsts", and that means you'll have to accept looking clumsy, maybe even stupid, but that's the story of most normal people when they first try something new. Don't be naïve enough to believe your best work will be your first attempt. So this book is my first attempt. That should come with the understanding that it might not be my best, but there is no way I'll get better without creating it.

Writing this book has been scary, stressful, anxiety-filled, but it has also been exhilarating, liberating and has filled me with pride because I have decided to act upon an unfulfilled desire that has haunted me for far too long.

Fill your life with firsts. Please don't waste your life in fear of other people's opinions. Let your memories be filled with "I did it!" and not "I wish I had". There is only sadness found in the latter.

Lesson 40

NEVER LOSE SIGHT OF THE BIRD IN THE HAND

I don't think that I'm the only person that thinks about the old saying "A bird in the hand is worth two in the bush". I feel ashamed sometimes for not being as grateful as I should be for the things I have in my life, but to live in gratitude isn't always easy. I am generally healthy, I have a job, I have an amazing wife, great friends and family.

I have a lot of things that I should be incredibly grateful for; however, I want more. I want to feel more fulfilled, I want to make more money, I want to be better, stronger, smarter. Shouldn't it be ok for me to want these things? Isn't it the hunger for more that has driven mankind towards achievement? Can you be content and yet driven? Hasn't it always been that in trying to achieve more, that you put what you already have at risk?

I am constantly plagued by these thoughts, and because I have not achieved anything that is particularly noteworthy, shouldn't I feel justified that I have these feelings of inadequacy? I have conversations with friends all the time about wanting to be more than I am, and I get annoyed when I'm told that I should be grateful. I am not ungrateful! I am aware of the great things I have in my life, I just still believe that there can be more to my life than what currently exists, and these feelings create anxiety.

Something tells me that I am not alone. In life we generally think that there are only two ways of looking at things: good or bad, right or wrong, left or right. There is very little consideration that there can be duality; you can be grateful for what you have and seek more. There is an underlying assumption of greed if one wants more from life. The examples are endless in religious stories. The persecutor is always wealthy and the righteous humble or poor. The very cartoons we grew up on included characters that were wealthy and would almost always be evil (e.g. Lex Luther). No wonder we have a society where people normally believe that the wealthy must have ulterior motives.

My point is that to be desirous of more aligns you psychologically with being evil. Some of the best people I have met in my life have done well for themselves. They are not obsessed with world domination, but are driven to create the life that they dream of for themselves and their families. There's a saying "the rich think both, the poor think either or".

The key is to never lose sight of the bird in hand, that is, all the things of value that you already have in your life. But be willing to push yourself towards being more, because there is nothing more boring and unfulfilling than stagnation.

Lesson 41

THE GREATER GOOD SHOULD ALWAYS INCLUDE YOU

I am an emotional person and so I have leaned hard into logical thinking to influence my decision-making process. Unfortunately for me, logic doesn't always win. I am fairly confident that how I process makes me a utilitarian: the decision made should benefit the greatest number of people. The problem is that in making those decisions to benefit the greatest number of people involved somehow I would choose not to count myself. In my mind, there has always been honour in self-sacrifice and so that's how I chose to live. Needless to say, quite often, it left me feeling unhappy.

It wasn't until I discovered Game Theory that I understood that if you are attempting to make the most logical decision for all parties involved, you are obligated to make the best decision for everyone involved, including yourself. It might sound silly to you, but for me it changed everything, I had been given a logical reason to think about myself and it was very liberating. It is your life, how could you possibly go through it not thinking about yourself? No one else is obligated to think about you or your feelings, so as a part of your own survival (it sounds dramatic, but it really isn't), you should endeavour to influence your environment to create favourable conditions for your existence.

The greater good should always include you, even if it involves some self-sacrifice, the benefits of making that sacrifice should outweigh the cost of your personal sacrifice.

Lesson 42

BE GENTLE WITH YOURSELF

I had the privilege of talking to a hospital chaplain recently. I had so many questions to ask her because so much of her life's work was interacting with people at the end of their lives and having to comfort their loved ones in the process. She was so full of life and energy and I asked her how she was able to not take the emotions associated with the tragedy of end-of-life home with her. She told me she did a lot of praying, she sought regular counselling for herself, she walked and meditated often.

The last question I asked her was what advice she could give me on life. She gave me three things:

1. Live – enjoy your life, give it all you've got
2. Connect – connect with your loved ones because they are the ones that will be there when your health starts to fade

3. Be gentle with yourself – you will make mistakes, you will hurt people and even yourself. But you are here to live, and it is all a part of living

I listened intently to what she said and promised myself that going forward it would be the way I approach the rest of my life regardless of what may come my way. Life is so fickle. We are here today and gone tomorrow, and if we would all truly recognize our mortality, we wouldn't waste a single moment on hate, malice, contempt or anger. We were given the opportunity to live, to find joy, to make love, to cherish our loved ones, to chase our passions. Everything else is inconsequential!

Lesson 43

YOUR FEELINGS AREN'T ALL THAT VALID

I have seen and been a part of many situations personally and professionally where I watched people indulge their emotions surrounding an issue to the point that they lose sight of what is actually taking place. Even in the face of evidence to the contrary they still "feel" that they have been wronged or that their feelings should still be validated. No one is obligated to indulge your emotions when you have chosen to continue to feel negative emotions although the facts state otherwise.

Misunderstandings are inevitable, but it's important to be able to get over yourself. The difficulty for most people is that they allow their ego to get so caught up with specific emotions, that once their feelings are challenged with verifiable information, they immediately attempt to skew the information in an attempt to continue to corroborate their feelings.

This only ends up making you look incapable of separating your emotions from the issue at hand, so the observer begins to view you as self-absorbed, immature and probably less intelligent than they thought before.

You never gain favour from indulging your emotions too much. To the observer you become more difficult to deal with because situations require so much more energy to bring you to a place of being able to identify that it's not about you. Human beings are emotional creatures by default, and it's not a bad thing to be emotional. Our emotions are the main drivers behind our desires to be, do or achieve anything. However, you have to be willing to take a step back and acknowledge that your feelings aren't always valid.

Lesson 44

DON'T MARGINALIZE YOUR GIFTS

It usually feels pretty good to come to the realization that you're good at something whether it's sports, academics, or the arts. And being acknowledged for being exceptional is fantastic! The problem with being naturally good at something is that there is a tendency to discount its value because you may feel as if you have not earned the right to claim it as a gift or you might downplay your gift because you assume that everyone else should have the same natural ability.

For example, if you're naturally good at math, you might have difficulty appreciating why other people aren't. But your gifts are no less than those of the people that you admire. Unfortunately, society tends to assign greater value to the gifts that can be monetized, such as being great at basketball, or being a financial wizard. But if your gift is poetry, do not discount it because society hasn't assigned it significant monetary value. Be the best poet you can be, explore your art, publish your work. You have no idea by whom, when or where your greatness will be acknowledged, and if not, know that at the very least you gave yourself the opportunity to create your masterpiece. There are enough people ready to tell you what you aren't good at, what you can't be or do. Don't listen of them. Don't ever marginalize your gifts.

Lesson 45

SOMETIMES EVEN YOUR FRIENDS WANT TO KNOW THAT YOU CAN FEEL PAIN

A mentor once told me, "If I cut off all my friends that have wronged me, I'd have no friends". We are imperfect creatures. We are capable of immense love and compassion, and we are also capable of incredible jealousy and envy. Unfortunately the latter can come from the people that we love the most.

I've been having some really honest conversations with friends. As we've gotten older, it feels like we've gotten closer to accepting our flaws and understanding even more that we are only human. We make mistakes and sometimes our thoughts betrayed us. We've been around long enough to see businesses start and fail, marriages begin and fall apart, some children raised to become amazing young adults and others misguided. The passage of time has a way of becoming a great equalizer, but most of us understand this too late. We will not all rise at the same time, and unfortunately some of us will fall, as is the nature of things. It is difficult to accept that as you grow, develop and achieve, some who love you would hope to see you fail; maybe not significantly, but just enough that they can either identify with you (having failed at something) or just to know that you aren't living a charmed life.

Jealousy can rear its ugly head and turn people who were once great friends into enemies. The challenge is in the acceptance of the fact that your friends at some point may be jealous of you for some reason or the other: marriage looking successful, business thriving, financial and material possessions increasing. Whatever it is, the fact of the matter is that their jealousy isn't about you, it's completely about their own feelings of inadequacy, and their perceived inability to change the situation for the better. It's a hard pill to swallow, to forgive a friend that clearly would like to see you fail. But remember that the jealousy and envy is about their own feelings of inadequacy.

We don't get to choose the flaws of the people we love, sometimes loving them is about the acceptance of those flaws. They are still your friend, just not in the ideal way that you wish they would be. They are only projecting their deficiency onto your proficiency. Forgive them, take pride in the fact that you are living a life that even those that love you could envy.

PART 5

Lesson 46

IT'S GOOD TO HAVE OTHERS BELIEVE IN YOU, BUT IT'S BETTER TO BELIEVE IN YOURSELF

I believe in cultivating a support system. It's wonderful to have people who see, believe and encourage your potential. For most of my life I tried to find my people, the people that would forever be a source of inspiration when times get tough. I found them, but then I realized that having others believe in me would never be enough for me to realize my potential, I had to believe in myself first.

Every time that I decided to embark on a new journey, there was never any movement until I could find it within myself to take the first step. It has always been hard, and I assume that it's the same for everyone else.

We all know that evolution is challenging. To be better than you were the day before will always require you to push harder than you pushed before. No amount of encouragement from anyone else can ever move you beyond your current state of being. It always has to come from within. The quicker you acknowledge that is the quicker you will be in a position to move towards your goals.

Men and women lesser than you have achieved great things by simply resolving in their minds that they will achieve a goal, and then taking action. The greatest difference has been and always will be self-belief. Every single time that I have been stagnated by the fear of pursuing a goal, it is when I come to the realization that the only thing standing in my way is me, that I am able to make the necessary steps towards achieving it. More often than not, I am annoyed with myself for not making the move earlier, mostly because no goal is ever as daunting as perceived. The fear of my own inadequacy can have paralyzing effect, but it is only through action that I will ever know whether or not my inadequacy is real.

I want to encourage you to pursue any and everything that's of interest to you. I know my words will mean nothing until you chose them to. It's good to have others believe in you, but it's better to believe in yourself.

Lesson 47

SOME PEOPLE SHOULD NEVER BE RAISED ABOVE THEIR STATION

Not all soldiers make great generals, so too not all associates make great friends. Kingdoms have been lost because emperors have elevated men who then gained the power to usurp their throne. Your life, your world, is your kingdom. Guard its gates and let no one who isn't truly deserving of your time, attention, and affections through. Never fall in love with the potential of a person. Ensure that there is proof of their abilities before you make any decisions to bring them closer to you.

We have all seen admirable qualities in people, potential that draws us in; quite often qualities that we see in ourselves and would like to encourage, because we wish others had given us the same opportunity. Be wary, some people should never be raised above their station. Whether personally or professionally, be guided by what people actually do. Never romanticize the relationship in order to validate the emotions that you have decided to assign to the interaction. Those feelings, emotions or even loyalty that you hope to gain may never be returned.

Some people are only there for what they can gain or achieve through an association or relationship. Remember that all that is given is happily received by a taker. There is no reciprocity. There is no allegiance to be gained, only an emptying of your coffers mentally, physically and emotionally. Keep your eyes open and your mind sharp. Failure to do so will intreat the succubus and incubus.

Lesson 48

BEING YOU MIGHT BE THE HARDEST DECISION YOU'LL EVER HAVE TO MAKE

So much of who we become is due to parental, societal and peer group pressure. If you take the time to try to strip away who you've been told to be, you might find it difficult to identify how much of "you" actually exists. If discovering who you truly are is of interest to you, it might take years to sieve through the expectations and the cultural norms that have shaped your being. I have friends who have walked away from lucrative professions to pursue their passions which may be far less financially stable but bring far greater joy to their lives.

Consider for a moment the millions of people that have lived and died never once having the opportunity to engage in discovering who they truly were because they were too busy living the lives that were expected of them. Does that idea of your life sit right with you? If it does that's fine, but if it doesn't, then I believe that at the very least you are obligated to try to discover who you truly are.

One of the best things that I have learned is that I don't have to be any one thing; whether it is my career, my character, my passions, no path has to be absolute. We have been put here to live, I would rather live a life of focusing on identifying who I am rather than who I am expected to be. You can too, if you so choose. Understand that if you choose a path of self-discovery that it will not be easy, it might even require you to remove people that you love from your life, not because they are good or bad, but the core of who you truly are would not have chosen them for your circle.

Being you might be the hardest decision you'll ever have to make, but it can also be the most fulfilling experience of your life as you become closer to self. It has never really been about life's journey; it has always been your journey.

Lesson 49

IT IS ONLY IN SOLITUDE THAT YOU CAN TRULY FIND YOURSELF

I had mentioned in an earlier chapter that I have always struggled with my weight. While doing my Master's degree I blew up to 350 lb. My diet was terrible, I slept very little, my stress level was through the roof, not only because of school, but there was a period in which I hadn't worked for several months. The only thing that kept me going was the thought that if I was just able to finish this degree that my job prospects would improve.

Shortly after finishing school I got a job as a Sales Manager. As I got dressed for work one day, I remember looking in the mirror and feeling very sad. How had I allowed myself to gain so much weight? How was I even going to lose the weight? I felt like it was going to be too daunting a task to get the weight off, and maintain it. I approached this situation as I had with every other problem I had endured in my life. I attacked it head on.

I decided to go on a low carb diet, cut out sugar, started back at the gym (my best friend actually paid the first month for me, because I hadn't yet gotten back on my feet financially). I walked 30 minutes a day for cardio (at my then weight, running was impossible). I spent a lot of time trying to visualize how I wanted to look and more importantly feel about myself.

I worked out with a couple of different people, which was great for getting ideas, but no one was on the mission I was on. I wanted more than just getting back to where I once was. I wanted to see my abdominal muscles, which meant that I'd have to engage in new exercises and have the mindset that they were all crucial to my new mission.

I'd get up at 4:30 a.m. so I could get to the gym and get a two hour workout in before work. There were times that I felt incredibly alone. I couldn't talk to anyone about it, because I was the one who did this to myself, again. I found strength and purpose in the daily challenges I gave myself to try new exercises. It felt incredibly rewarding to realize that I was not only capable of doing some of the exercises at my size, but that I excelled at them. To keep myself accountable, I recorded and posted tons of videos to Instagram to keep me honest. I figured if I started slacking off, someone would notice and let me know.

It worked!... I worked out no less than 5 days a week for two years straight. I lost 80 lb and had gained significant muscle mass.

I liked how I looked and felt. I was aware that I still had more work to do, but I was incredibly proud of myself for stepping up for me and doing what needed to be done to regain the confidence that I had lost. The greatest lesson I learned was that throughout my entire life, whenever I wanted to do something, it was in solitude that I was able to find myself. Family, friends and well-wishers can cheer you on and offer amazing support, but at the end of the day, you are the one who has to do the work. The only way you'll ever be able to move the needle forward is through belief in self, determination, self-respect, consistency, a clear vision and empathy. For every failure I've had in my life, there is also a story of triumph, because there is an indelible self-belief that comes from the core of my being, which has always been found in time spent in solitude.

Lesson 50

WHERE THERE IS CONFLICT, THE ANSWER SHOULD BE YES

I've always been a very confrontational person, whether it was because of an argument or if it was because I was standing up for what I believed to be right. What that led to most of the time was an escalation of the situation which could have been avoided. I'd often feel stupid after a confrontation because I realized that I could have handled myself better, or even avoided the situation all together if I had taken stock of the entire interaction and more importantly, how insignificant it was in many cases.

I would often get so emotionally invested in the defence of my position that I wouldn't even let myself be open to the opposing argument. But if I am going to engage someone, then I should at least be willing to listen to what they have to say. The initial disagreement would at times spiral into a whole different argument because of the language and tone used.

It took me years to learn, and I am still learning, that where there is conflict, the answer should be yes. What this means is that when someone presents you with an argument, if you disagree or think it makes no sense, saying “yes” gives you the opportunity to try to see the other person’s perspective, and opens you up to hearing what is truly being communicated. At the very least, what happens is that you allow the other person the space to be heard, and your “yes” whether verbal or suggested, immediately eliminates the possibility of there even being conflict. Then when you choose to speak, what happens is that you are sharing your perspective which won’t have to be received as a rebuttal or counter argument.

Remember, if it is that you truly want to be heard and possibly change someone else’s perspective, conflict/confrontation rarely if ever leads to agreement. The only way to truly lay siege to one’s ego is to placate it.

Lesson 51

IF YOU'RE AFRAID OF CHANGE, THEN YOU'RE AFRAID OF LIVING

For a very long time I have been trying to figure out how to articulate my feelings about change, in particular the acceptance of it. I have noticed that most people that I interact with will respond to change with anger. I've never quite understood it because in my mind what value is there in getting angry. Life happens, things don't work out, things get broken. These are just what I like to think of as symptoms of life, and what you have to decide to do is treat the symptoms. I am not suggesting that it is always easy to accept; however, how you choose to respond invariably determines how quickly your life or situation will re-stabilize.

You can waste so much energy resisting change that you can end up disrupting your life and even your livelihood. I have watched people get so caught up in their egos that they lose sight of the fact that the situation being faced might not even be about them. There might be a greater good to be considered, but they develop a form of tunnel vision related to the situation that makes it completely personal for them, and that leads to disruptive behaviour.

If we were all to truly accept the inevitability of change, then the ability to navigate the challenges posed would increase tenfold by virtue of our adaptability. If you're afraid of change then you're afraid of living. Try to imagine a world that never changes and you'll see a world that collapses. Wouldn't you rather be on the side of those that choose to adapt rather than those who are weighed down by what once was? The freedom found in one's ability to adapt can only be experienced by he who chooses to remain fluid in the face of change.

Lesson 52

THOUGH THE JOURNEY FEELS LONELY, NONE OF US WALK ALONE

My father often says, "If men were to all put their problems in a pot together, they'd take back their problems quickly". This essentially means that what we're going through is never as bad as we think. I consider myself fortunate to have an amazing support system and even though I know it, I often feel alone. I live in my head, constantly processing my world, what actually exists, what I would like to change, what I would like to change in me.

If you're anything like me, then you'll often feel alone, because no matter what, it is your journey of life, and no one can take it for you. However, we are far less different from each other than we'd like to think. We all experience similar emotions, share passions, hopes, dreams, and even crises. The more time you spend talking to people, genuinely getting to know them, the more you'll realize that we are all just trying to figure out our individual place in the world.

Whether you're incredibly financially successful or financially desolate, there is something within the human spirit that consistently seeks to be or feel more. Strip everything away and what exists is a need to connect, to be a part of something greater. If we could all realize that then we'd live in a much better world where a sense of community would exist, where our value would be defined through our contribution to society and not what we seek to hoard for ourselves. Many have sought to fill the void with material things, and because they are easy to place a value on, we define them as valuable. We are a lost society, devoid of what truly matters... love.

"How can I help?". In my daily life I use this phrase often, and it opens me up to being a part of another person's experience and gives me a sense of fulfilment after making a difference in another person's day. Even saying the words brings a smile to my face because it already acknowledges that I have value, because I can make a difference. So I remind myself every day, though the journey feels lonely, none of us walks alone.

Lesson 53

REFLECTION

If the story is true, that when you die God shows you who you could have been, I'm pretty confident that I'll be going to hell. I am incredibly aware that I could have been so much more, achieved so much more with my life, been greater than I am. I chose to play it small for most of my life, whether it was due to my shyness, my introversion, myself doubt or possibly even my difficulty with the identification of a passion or vision.

As I write this very line, I am still struggling with my place in the world and still struggling with my self-limiting thoughts. I am still uncertain whether there is any greatness that I can achieve in my life. It is painful. It is torturous. It is life. I am not consoled by the fact that many others grapple with these thoughts, for there are those that have achieved far more than I that share my beliefs, and there are those that have achieved far less and still share my fate.

The beauty, I believe is in the fact that those consistent, nagging thoughts that we can all be more and do more have propelled humans from the beginning of time towards growth and development as a species. You are unhappy with who you are because you believe that you can be more, and you can be more because you are unhappy with who you are. It is a never-ending cycle.

Choose every day to try to be more than you were the day before, chase that best version of yourself, ignore the naysayers because they know nothing of who you truly are or can be, and remember that you are the only person that gets to determine if you are winning at life. I hope when you go to hell that you will still be able to smile, because none of us will ever be absolutely all we could have been, but you did everything possible to find out. Take it from a loser, you're already winning at life.

THE END

TABLE OF LESSONS

How To Win At Life

Work Hard... And Then Let People Know You Did

It's Ok To Play Scared

In Times Of Struggle, You Can Still Find Beauty

You're Going To Spend A Lot More Days Working Than Celebrating

You Can't Pour From An Empty Cup

You Are Not An Imposter

The Fear Of Failure Is Never Good Enough A Reason Not To Try

Get Comfortable Talking About Money

When You Feel An Itch, Scratch It

Even The Good You Do Is Still About You

You Become Who You Choose To Be Through Repetition

Make Adversity Your Friend

Embrace Your Greatest Fear

Release The Disappointments Of The Past

Find A Healthy Outlet

Feel The Betrayal, Forgive Quickly

Free Your Mind From Self-Limiting Thoughts

Even When You're Lost, You're Still Somewhere

Don't Be Naïve Enough To Believe Your Best Work Will Be Your First Attempt

Never Lose Sight Of The Bird In The Hand

The Greater Good Should Always Include You

Be Gentle With Yourself

Your Feelings Aren't All That Valid

Don't Marginalize Your Gifts

Sometimes Even Your Friends Want To Know That You Can Feel Pain

It's Good To Have Others Believe In You, But It's Better To Believe In Yourself

Some People Should Never Be Raised Above Their Station

Being You Might Be The Hardest Decision You'll Ever Have To Make

It Is Only In Solitude That You Can Truly Find Yourself

Where There Is Conflict, The Answer Should Be Yes.

If You're Afraid Of Change, Then You're Afraid Of Living

Though The Journey Feels Lonely, None Of Us Walk Alone

Reflection

www.ingramcontent.com/pod-product-compliance
Lightning Source LLC
LaVergne TN
LVHW010610160826
845677LV00013B/3341

* 9 7 9 8 3 5 1 7 4 2 7 1 7 *